Falling
Machinations of My Mind

by

Pim

DORRANCE
PUBLISHING CO
EST. 1920
PITTSBURGH, PENNSYLVANIA 15238

Dorrance Publishing Co
585 Alpha Drive
Pittsburgh, PA 15238
Visit our website at *www.dorrancebookstore.com*

ISBN: 978-1-6495-7303-2
eISBN: 978-1-6495-7323-0

FALLING

Losing pieces of hope as you fall into a deeper
depression knowing you don't know how to fix it. You
fall with a rope next to you, but just like in the dream
you know what you are supposed to do, but you just
stare at it blankly because you can't tell your body to
move even though your brain is telling you to

I feel the madness creeping on up in me
The demons create blindness
They are the ones that can see
Spiral
Hitting no high notes
Feels like I'm continuously getting hit in the scrotes

The rope that is behind me it strokes
I dream about the days of the past
Storks
I want to forgive everyone
Yet, they challenge me to take them to court
Yet, all I want is the "no girls allowed" fort
Yet, before I know it, I'll be fore-tee
Yelling, no please
Give me one more chance
Let me go back, you see
It was like Adam Sandler in Click
I am living remotely
Oh, please
No hoes, you see
I lived my life with little to no sin, geez

I am consumed from the madness
Creating new fads,
Unless, I let the darkness take over me
The demons look down on me
Taking control
Watching as I freefall or flee
Not facing anything head on
No, please
Just let time freeze
I beg you,
I'm on my knees.

No, you don't see
The darkness that clouds you is eating your life away
Yet, you just sit there and wallow day after day.
You can't see there is rain
Clearly the mist is giving your nipples a nice little
    twist and you just give up.
No, please keep fighting, it is what causes the
    demons to fear you.
Please save yourself
I saved my life
I want you to be able to say
#metoo.

"Wake me up when my reality is better than my fantasy"
That's how they get ya,
You want it to be brought to you
Yet what have you proved?
What did you do?
I can make art with macaroni
See, go shove it
I'm great at life
Jabroni.

People will always put you down
People will pull a fast one
Look like a clown
They are gonna make you look like you have an
      extra chromosome
Downs.
You show them the best you
Turn it around.
Next year, shit's gonna go down.
My shackles are free
Please listen to my journey
Don't be afraid to join
It costs a little coin
You will grow
And get a hairy groin.
If not, you can just be poignant.
Give all the demons ointment
After you are done leaving them in the dust, thrown
      out and abandoned
They are going to need it
Burn of the tires and the burns on them.

I am set free
I am happy as can be
Rhymes they come quite easily
If you follow me and you are blind
Then I will show you that you can shine
Loneliness is a burden
The demons they are slowly murderin'
The relationships you will have
They will cheat
And someone else will get them squirtin'
If you choose to stay blind
Then you stay with your own kind
My mind is shrill
Let us get rid of the demons
Let's go kill
12 hours to go
No rules
Kill the demons
Go
Oh, no.

"Wake me up when my reality is better
        than my fantasy"
That's how they get ya,
You want it to be brought to you
Yet, what have you proved?
What did you do?
I can make art with macaroni
See, go shove it
I'm great at life
Jabroni.

Japanese Three

I want to be seen
through a child's eye
They do not lie
Unlike the 3 faces you've seen before
They only have one
No less, no more
We always find it a sore.
Unknown to blood and gore.
They stand by who they want
They don't keep track of score
They see who is really underneath
What others perceive
They try to say p-p-p
Perceive no more.
Not a child
I am Immortalized, Nevermore.

I am hated by all the adults
The kids really know me
The children will show me
They don't know what's right and wrong
Only what they see
They are not covered up
By the Japanese three.
The shields we use to hide from the adults
Can't be hidden by children
They could save our lives
Like epinephrine
Instead of choking
They let us breathe
Lest we give into our selfish minds
Our other voices
Or the impossible quench of our greed.

What you see is what others want to see
They don't know the true me
The haters are evil and gree-dy
I will not immortalize
They do get to me
I can't just let them win
Go ahead call me grea-zy
They can't be a carbon copy
Then again in my eyes
Who would want to be?
As we get older, we close our mind
Have to go to work
Have to hit this grind
All while looking for yourself
It is hard to find
Who we truly were
Were the children we see

We grow up and that's what we need
A new life
We can raise them, see
The life is all brought out
The vision you can see
When you're with your kids
You are less blinded by the Japanese 3
They bring out your inner child once again
But the responsibilities there is no end
Instead of the children that seek me
They love me
I want to find a different way to lose the masks
        that have tortured me.
Adventure and wonder
Where did that go?
Only to lose the best part of me.

What you see is what others refuse to
They don't know the true me
The haters are evil and gree-dy
I will not immortalize
They do get to me
I can't just let them win
Go ahead call me grea-zy
They can't be a carbon copy
Then again in my eyes
Who would want to be?
Innocence brought about
Adventure and wonder
Where did that go,
No! Don't leave
Japanese Three
The mask is no longer me

COMPLETELY INCOMPLETE

I know what I do
I mess up
I screw up too
Nothing but mistakes
And undercut
Am I through?
Hearing the calls
Come back,
HI, I'm Paul
To be complete is to be on the other side
However, the gap is 3 meters wide.
Keep me here
Another puff
And I glide.

Smoking is something I never thought of
    myself doing
My life is confusing
I am construing
I am completely fuming
I let myself do this?
Tell me why you did it
Thesis
No thanks
These are done
I've hit my final road
Maybe the princess will
Finally notice this ugly toad
Man, why do I crave rocky road?

I know that the stereotype exists
I'm not out there banging chicks
I feel my confidence rise
I take first prize
It brings back the old me
The one full of innocence
And no trophies
Where participation wasn't put so high
Damn it, it makes me want to cry

I know that we get stuck in the past
The memories of us will forever last
You don't want to relive memories
Until you're gassed
Live in the moment before the moment has passed
I know it's typical to hear
I just want you to know
Life goes fast.

I know that what I do is wrong
Maybe I need an icepick or a couple of prongs
I don't understand why whale tails are so wrong
I just don't know why you want a UTI and wedgie.
Why'd they have to kill off Neij?
Man, I don't want a Reggie.
The mistakes I made are what made me
Take me to the past and find the past of what
    I have become
Ignorance is bliss
It doesn't make me dumb.
I just want to be away from the pain
I just want to live life happily
Don't want to explain.
The pain in life
I just want to be numb.
Where did real life even come from?

I know that we get stuck in the past
The memories of us will forever last
You don't want to relive memories
Until you're gassed
Live in the moment before the moment has passed
I know it's typical to hear
I just want you to know
Life goes fast.

OPEN

You want to claim my love and your fame.
The love and affection
All of you sound the same.
He is who he is
I am still molding.
The cards you both have
You are folding.

He is who he is
You see what you want
What you see in him is perfection
What you see in me is flawed
He is perfect in your eyes
He does no wrong.
What he does is always right
What I do is always wrong
The words he spit are music to your ears
Yet, all you see in me is a flaw.
You went behind me and talked to the law
Stabbed in the back
You used a claw?

He is who he is
Not a flaw in sight
You are blinded by the love
In spite.
Everyone sees but you
That relationship
Complete shite.
Yet, what you see in me
Get away
Take flight.

All I want is love and affection.
Acceptance and a nod
You play with my mind
Like you are my god.
Toy with me more
Twisted and demented I get
The more you fuck me up
The more I want to slit. (Worthless, stupid, a
fucking cunt, man, I regret you, you are not my son)

I can't sleep at night
The words you say give me such a fright.
As the sun comes up and my eyes get heavy,
The beast sleeps
Fight or flight
Bitch, you ain't ready.
(Unscrewed
Not a couple of screws
The voices tell me
I want to kill you.)

I write what I write
It's so heavy
When they leave my fingers
I feel so light.
Right into his arms you go
The only thing I have
Is this heavy-ass flow
That's what you made me
Silent and still
No wonder I can't sleep
I take these pills.

I have these gills because the water isn't drowning
As I gasp for air.
You kill me
Willingly.
If you bring that responsibility on me
You won't see what he becomes
I'll be the devil you always claimed me to be.
Too bad, number 3
Your heart won't beat.

This is me
Featuring me
All I can see
Is my MPD
Dissociate
Obliterate
Confiscate.
Sight will be
I can't say it to your face
I am no longer afraid
I put my head down
Shame
By the time you see my success
I'll be long gone and dead to you
Mentally, I am prepared
Soon, you will lose your hair.
Not from chemo
Or from age.
2 years
You will be rotting away.

Make amends to who you can.
Cologne is your best attempt?
You will be unkempt

All I want is love and affection.
Acceptance and a nod
You play with my mind
Like you are my god.
Toy with me more
Twisted and demented I get
The more you fuck me up
The more I want to slit. (Worthless, stupid, a
fucking cunt, man, I regret you, you are not my son)

I can't sleep at night
The voices keep me awake.
I have so many different versions of me
Which one is writing it and which one will read?
Does this make my writing from a ghost writer?
Or am I just cheating?
Which ones claim and which ones are me?

One session and I'm told I am crazy
As professional as she can say it
I'm not stupid
I have wit.
One more time
Cutting the ties.
Making one more slit.

I write what I write
It's so heavy
When they leave my fingers
I feel so light.
Right into his arms you go
The only thing I have
Is this heavy-ass flow
That's what you made me
Silent and still
No wonder I can't sleep
I take these pills.

(Unscrewed, worthless,
Not a couple of screws, stupid, a fucking cunt, the
voices tell me,
The voices tell me, man, I regret you, you are not
my son, I want to kill you. Thoughts begun, voices
begone, Minecraft mod, I am god)
Silence

As it quiets down
What is more unnerving.
That they won't stop
Or they stop going?
Anticipate
Obliterate
This I cannot take

CURSE

Before I start this, I want to say I love you, and that I
    wish you could understand what I am trying to say.
This is difficult
Please find forgiveness on the way

You love me to no end
Life I am unable to fend off
People just look at me and scoff
Toff-ee
You are addicted to the caffeine
Coff-ee

You loved me to no end
Confrontation I cannot defend
Protecting me left me unprotected
My place in life is untouched and uncontested
I want you to know that I felt blessed
Now I know it was wrong
I suffocated
Now I am stressed
I have barely mated
I feel all or none
Trying to figure this out
I feel constipated
I feel untrained
All I feel is strain.
Life is just a pain
What I have done with my time is lame

You used to tell me what to do
"Look and nod, if he asks you anything just say,
'I don't know,' you understand what I am saying?"
I see, but what should I start believing?
Staying quiet has me seething
My feelings are unrelenting
Death row is pending

CRIPPLE

I know since the age of 10
I was still different then
Always hated English
Have to put down the pen
What am I gonna do?
How am I gonna do it?
When?

A knife to my head
My sister pries it out
I was an eight-year-old Boy Scout
I just sit here and pout
My tears they end this drought
Who knew the holes I had to fill?
The problems I have would mold me better
Grout

I knew the problems would never end
My days would forever spend
The spiral of insanity
I picked the pen up
I can't stand it, you see
It's what matters to me

I would yearn for the day
To waste away
Something to believe
I thought it was fabricated
Fake like a weave
You act like someone else
Put on a new persona
Just another clon-
Uh, another to own uh-
Please show me the way
I know that this is the day
I can finally say

My life is brought here
I was pulled back
Held by a spear
Didn't know I had everything to fear
Yet, still gotta steer.
Pull myself up
It hurts, but not my peers
Yet, how did this happen
What did the voices say?
What did they hear?
I think what I know now is absurdly clear

Do you ever wonder what death would be?
Naturally you think there is something special
You do right and there is nothing to fear
Yet, when I was six
I was ready to die
It was merely there
Outer space I would leer

Can you imagine, death by steer?
Game over
He is here.
We are brains with vessels
I want to create like Russel
With my emotions I just tussle
When I was younger, I was told not to wrastle.
I had wished that death came in bundles
I was so jealous of Michael
Dying, I might hold
The grudge for a while.
Real rap is out of style
I just want to whistle to my own tune
I don't want to hire no goons
I may not be no Hop
I don't care how rich or famous I get
I just want my album to drop
Maybe I'll be cream of the crop
"Man, you can just stop"
See, now I don't know what's going on
I feel like life is a game and I am just a chess pawn
Playing the wrong game in the right way
Maybe I'll play the right game in the wrong way.

Is it crazy that my demons went from outside of me
To being my eyes
The only ones that can see
Living inside
I'll fight like Creed
Now that I've banished them from the inside,
    they manifest into people
They want to trample me
I just keep them locked in the steeple
Those are people
They are weeple.
Just a clone of the next demon who tries to
    keep hold of me.
They know I am too strong to keep holding
My father spent his whole life scolding.
My aura never died
So, I kept on going.

Do you ever wonder what death would be?
Naturally you think there is something special
You do right and there is nothing to fear
Yet, when I was six
I was ready to die
It was merely there
Outer space I would leer

In high school I had to present
The worst thing ever
It was coy
Fuck, please no, god, no,
I don't want to go
Next is me
What will they think of me?
Thump, thump
Under the boards
He still breathes
Maybe that's my sanity
Dwindling to nothing
There has got to be something.
Pry it out
Fuck the new "Boy Scouts"
Feminazis
You run around with let the blood flow
Gross
Put it away
Nobody wants to smell your fish get stabbed and gutted
God, and here I was about to have nutted
Take a shower
Maybe you won't smell like Hitler and mustard.
That's okay, I know what you need
Genocide is the only way to please the gods
The virgin sacrifices have all gathered
Now you are talking about vegans and feminism being one?
If we eradicated them, we will have won
Trump is here?
Oh, fuck, we really done.
At this rate
I don't want a son

Imagine knowing you want to die for 15 years
Crying all of your tears
Letting the fears
Control you
Own you
PWN you
Your father disowns you
No wonder I'm a Debbie downer
Only for Christmas I'm Mister Scrooge.

Do you ever wonder what death would be?
Naturally you think there is something special
You do right and there is nothing to fear
Yet, when I was six
I was ready to die
It was merely there
Outer space I would leer

Past Me and Future

The fight I pursue
Is what I've needed to come to
The past me and the future
I smoke to keep both intact,
But in the process, I lose part of me
I can only keep one nostalgia
Or the right to be my full, potentially
Critically making blows knowing I have nothing left to show
To prove that I like what I like in the past
I feel like life can fuck me
However, when I want to fuck life back and take control of me
I feel like I'm on a strangling virtue
Chastity, I have finally met you
The journey is long and winding

I have 3 sights and the third eye is opened
What does that mean?
I can see the past and future me
Yet what I can't do
Is continue to be me
Fantasize won't help
It's what locks us as a whole
That's why the one percent has claimed the population as we
We the people
To stay a sheeple
Keep us in the steeple
Until we get old and we weep ol' days need to come back

We just needed to pick up our own slack
Free and easy
Everyone is sleazy
Yet what I find crazy is opening the third eye
Is helpful and dangerous
It's make or break
We need to turn to us
Open our full potential
Go into our mind's central
Hit all the doubters with the Kelvin stand still.
Mr. Freeze and Captain Cold
They know what I mean
Stop! You fiend
Just become a we
And take another pill.
That's your only will.

The past me loved the gaming industry
In some ways I still do
I can't deny that, it's true
Smash me, bro
No homo
You can be Link and I'll be Zelda.
Actually, I like the doctor way more
Lose until I even the score.
Yet, what bothers me is I don't even play it
anymore.

Not that I still don't love the game
But I miss the old smash
Not this ultimate form
I just sit here and scorn
Then I lay back and mourn
This game is now foreign
I've fallen out of love
It's time to turn around
Take down the glove
And return to the present
I don't want to leave the game behind,
Yet, it has left me
Spiritually.

I am third eye opened
Yet, my progress is blind
What I want to be mine
Is eating me away because I'm not there
I'll force the Chastity and the world to be kind
I just hope I don't become someone else
I don't want to be the next to be lined up
Pistol shot
Life is a struggle and we kill it with letting time pass us by.

The future I see a famous artist
The next big thing
The next Eminem? No
The first and only me
I am deep in thought about what was wrong

No sex drive
No Mr. Wong
I have work ahead of me
I need to get hair back on my dong
I need to take chances
Write what is wrong.
Then suddenly it takes over
The demon.

I am third eye opened
Yet, my progress is blind
What I want to be mine
is eating me away, because I'm not there
I'll force the Chastity and the world to be kind
I just hope I don't become someone else
I don't want to be the next to be lined up
Pistol shot
Life is a struggle and we kill it with letting time
        pass us by.

Now, that makes me curious
While my third eye is still open before I close it and
        continue with my journey
Is a demon a Pokémon or Digimon?
I think personally it would have to be a Digimon
        because all of the Digimon monsters have
        money at the end.
So, from now on I'll consider the demons a
        Digimon and the devil a Pokémon, because
        Pokémon reign supreme over Digimon, hey, whatever

You can deny all you want, but what I stated was true.
 It's just fate. My third eye closes, no wait. I miss my
 past and I love what's happened.
I'll miss you, you'll be in my memories
When I pass you just wait
I'll make up for all the time I've
Wasted, and you'll have waited
When I pass us being together again is all but fated.
 I just know I'll have to use this serrated to
 separate us for now.
We will see each other again, I just don't know how.

VIVIDLY

I know I grow slow
Feel almost as low as techno
These times I just don't know
I just don't know if I glow
I see them gleaming
All the people beaming brighter than me
This life I'm not tried
This life can go die
I will not try
I will go and fly
Why wait this enormous time?
Tomorrow I might write my last line
I don't mean crack
I meant my punchline

I see through adversity
No, I don't need no University
I feel the tenacity
In the same way you act good, you see
You get the grades in school
This is what makes you happy
I like writing stories
Let you watch it through my words like a dream
You live it vividly
Your brain isn't dark, this might not be you
However, this is me.

I want to be so many things, we all agree
I wanted to be a wrestler, a ref, a QB, go be a psych
    major at a technically.
Now I want to make rhymes and get past the sadness
I want to work on the will of fire within my own agency.
    A metaphor for what's inside of me.
I create my own rules and my own life
Just because I follow the law doesn't mean I can't
    destroy a scene.
I just do it while you watch with your eyes closed.
    Again, watching it vividly.

I see through adversity
No, I don't need no University
I feel the tenacity
In the same way you act good, you see
You get the grades in school
This is what makes you happy
I like writing stories
Let you watch it through my words like a dream
You live it vividly
Your brain isn't dark, this might not be you
However, this is me.

You want to live as high as me?
Jump through hopes
Deal with a loss in the family
Even when they're gone-ily
Maybe that was too subtle
I just want you to know
I fully see

What you need from me
Keep your legacy alive
You made your mistakes and you made your past
You learned how to grow up at such a seasoned age.
Of course, you were still you
That's the era you grew into
You knew you had to change
Yet, you were still a stubborn old, man too.
The love you inspired in me
Should have been bestowed on your wife too.
She loved you through and through
Even with all that you did she still loved you just
    like mourning dew. She will have the next
    morning, thinking what should I do?

Your daughter shows what is quite frankly the
    better half of you
Showing love where no one should show love to.
If It weren't for her constant guidance and her love
    to be true.
I wouldn't even be thinking of doing this too.
I want the best part of me to be shown,
I just wish you loved them both and bestow the love
    on them just like you did to me
In the end it's not the destruction you create,
It is just the love you bestowed, what we have overcome
That goes to show my mother being dragged to nothing
    and feeling distant
I should have seen this coming
However, just like most stories, I missed it.
Sometimes life is over at an instant
Time to get the bread
Or if you want to call it,
I guess you could call it a biscuit.

FAREWELL

The night used to be hellish, dark and demented.
A heavy drought
I thought my life was cemented.
My ego should have been forever dented
Now I take happiness from the darkness
The demons try to dent it.
I want to create music
I meant it
We are all forms of art
The art of the smart
The art to push a cart?
Jackass, even an art to fart
Take this man's right to create a design
I can't taste the picture, but man, it feels like it
    would taste tart.
I feel like I'm evolving
I may not cure cancer
There isn't a way, I am cancerous
I do more than good
That's what matters is
I create good from the bad
Even when I am not glad
This is what is to be had
People see my successes and setbacks
Yet all they want from me is to keep me on their
    demented track
They can keep me down
I don't like that

You want me to just act flat
Making me eat my feelings
That's why I'm getting fat
I let you control me so much.
That's why right now life
Is soo rough.
I found the culprit
I'm like Scooby-Dooo
Everything comes back to me
Yet, what will I go through
A bit of brokeeen tools
Uh, I mean I wanna hit a couple fools
Muh life is renewed.

I know I can't sleep
These demons are crude
They found a new way to slow me down
System of a frown
They think they can keep me clowned
I couldn't write that much
I was no longer the clutch
Stuck in first gear
What is there to fear?
Good and kind
I don't want to be part of the blind leading the
blind.
I don't want to be sheep
Why do people still drive the gas-guzzling jeep?
I think that I've gotten some off my mind
I think it's time for my brain to rest and sleep.

The demons they want to attach
They get one last grasp and the last bit of ill will.
They still want to keep me down
I was born in the happiest of times
These will be strange lines
I started life great
Then it was a nightmare I couldn't escape
To become alive long enough to see me be the bad
guy
Then be so young to return to who I once was and
be the strong guy,
The happy little unknowing buzzing fly.
More knowledge from my guy.
This should be how life is always.
If life is supposed to be filled
Then when I overflow with happiness
All I can do is finding myself cry.
Farewell to doubt tonight, let my dreams give me
as close to a human's spiritual flight

CHAMBER "SLEEP WE(E)(A)K"

The negative effects of sleep, like the experiment
Insomnia is the way to our true selves.
The lack of sleep shows us our true nature
It shows us what our true being is
Our primal nomenclature
We can never hit such a thing
It is impossible
Yet the Russian experiment makes it plausible.

Prisoners of war
The gas they wanted more.
30 days of no sleep
Just to see what sleep is made for
Rapid eyes move
As we almost surface
The twilight it brings
Our true intentions almost never surface
Anything to stay awake
Friday, stay away from the lake
Killers and sociopaths
That's what it takes

These stories might not be true
However, there is sense made from this too.
The later we are awake
The more we let loose
As the morning comes, we are the swan
Swift and right, always trying to bring light.
As the night comes and the darkness rises, we
        become the goose
A goose that patronizes.
The few that show their true selves
Are ones that cannot sleep
Without making others' cuts
So extremely deep.
What will it take to push you over the edge?
Where are you?
Hiding behind that hedge?
Why do you escape the torments?
Arguing parents
Just to hear me say this?
I see that your window faces your backyard and you
        think you're safe
I stand back there waiting
You shouldn't pace
If I come up there and show you truth
All your smaller problems will just go poof.
Killing you is no fun
I won't let you go that easily
I don't know why people keep telling me to get cooped
Show me how I am crazy
Just run another loop.
What is the big scoop?
Just like Dairy Queen
Your life will get turned upside down
Once I show you the truth.
I want to stay wide awake
Show you true pain
Without this knowledge

You will never truly understand my disdain
Don't worry, soon you won't hear that train. You
won't get distracted
Your destiny will be in plane sight
Just ask A-Rod or Wainwright.
Hiding from the truth
While it is in plain sight
You see darkness in my actions
I see my actions in the streetlight
I am here to save you from yourself
Alright
Refuse to adhere to our calling, you won't end with
a guy, might.
There is no wrong or right
Just the actions that some find fearful
Some find fright.

If you agree to go with me, we will control our
destiny
Show other people the way to go
In our dim world we shall listen to Naomi
Let the darkness get swelled up with our glow.
Do you feel it?
Anyone who doesn't agree won't git and grow up
They will be our trophies to never stray
They, with our help, will stand up.
Sleep is for the weak
Yet, when they sleep, they sleep for a week.
They stay awake to avoid us
Yet, they will eventually sleep.
I'll show them what kind is deep.

UNKNOWN

I am the point in my life where I break free
Or continue to live poorly
The bridges I burn
They will happen continuously
Graciously given two talents
The talent to fuck up
Then the talent to write about it.
I am on the edge of success
Yet, I am on the verge of failing enormously
A crossroads to say
For the past 4 months I have been there
Like an itch,
Woof, woof
Sit and stay
How much longer can I live in this
Unorthodox way

I live inadequately
How do you live with undiagnosed Asperger's?
I'll tell you how I live life on the fray
How to save a life?
Okay

I torture myself daily
I hate to live with myself, frankly
The days I live I feel like a stray
How am I going to be happy, gay?
I feel like mystery meat
Served to everyone
Yet, only few will play
The dangerous game
Yet, I sit here and say
Stray from the path
Hear my words
Those words will touch your heart in a certain way

I live inadequately
A bitch to consider
My final days
When no one accepts me
How can I not do the same?
How do I stay on this Earth?
Confidently say
I will live to fight another day?

Life is worth cherishing
Life hates all that pass through
Coming out of the womb
It gives you an early tomb
You have to fight your way through the darkness
Life goes like a Cadillac
Zoom, zoom
Looking at a game called Doom

Dark souls rise above
The monsters you fight are the ones that are
fighting from above
They want to sweep you under
They want you to sit there and fumble
I just hear a lot of grumbles

They sit and laugh as you walk and stumble
You and I feel inadequate
Yet I write and I come out of it
Autistically artistic
The test comes true
You need to search for some blue clues.
Let your imagination free
Then maybe you will write as free
Willfully, yet artistic as can be.

How do I live one more day?
I drown out the people who patronize me
Tear me down
Telling me to be salty
Lays down
I rise above what they have to say

FATHER

You see what you see
It has never felt like you were a father to me
How can I ever amount to anything?
My father wants nothing to do with me
A family is supposed to be a unit
A collective of people who bring each other up
It seemed like you always thought of me as just a
    red Solo cup.
Used and then tossed to the side
As I try to win your love or attention
Blissful innocence wide-eyed
As I got older, I stopped sat still and silently cried
Dreaming of the days to get my angel wings
    and just fly.
I wish you saw me in my mama's eyes.

I see that you want to try
Love has no bounds
If God does exist
He wants that love to be blown sky high
Just as you try to make amends
I want to move away
Make my own trends
You have no idea why I strive
I've lived in fear since you feel dead inside
I finally feel alive.

Love is cruel

We were both part of depression's tools
I found my way
I fear that you will live blinded until your final day
So, as I sit here and sway to the words, I say
I pray that you find your own mind's heaven someday
One day you will stop smoking and drinking
I fear that day will be the day that life takes your
      final breath away.

The chance may be lost with me
However, you have another son you can take care of
If you feel like you will fail, do it for me
Time is no one's luxury
I just hope you stand
Unless all the fights you wind up losing the biggest
      fight to me
I don't want to fist fight, that's not what I mean
The mistakes you keep inside, they are mostly
      because of me.
As we both take fault
We need to pole vault and be civil
Why start a fight?
That would be so trivial.

Depression takes hold
There our characters will mold
The more complete we get
Being in the demon's grips
The harder it is to overcome
Yes, I am still the same son
The one that would amount to nothing
I have become strong
Shortcomings and all
I just don't want you to fall

Stand tall or rock bottom will make another call.
I just want you to be safe
Hitting your closed mind
Depression is blocking your subconscious wall

Love is cruel
We were both part of depression's tools
I found my way
I fear that you will live blinded until your final day
So, as I sit here and sway to the words, I say
I pray that you find your own mind's heaven someday
One day you will stop smoking and drinking
I fear that day will be the day that life takes your
    final breath away.

The chance may be lost with me
However, you have another son you can take care of
If you feel like you will fail, do it for me
Time is no one's luxury
I just hope you stand
Unless all the fights you wind up losing the biggest
    fight to me
I don't want to fist fight, that's not what I mean
The mistakes you keep inside, they are mostly
    because of me.
As we both take fault
We need to pole vault and be civil
Why start a fight?
That would be so trivial.

MINDSET

How you act depends on your age,
Fill your mind up with rage
The mind creates its own cage

You want to say that I don't know the feeling
Feel the age dissolve away
Your mind and body separate
Reminisce of the good old days
Of school lunches
With kids not having their phone in their face
Walk back and forth
Continue to pace
Nostalgia is laced
It will consume your very being
As you realize in this world you are leaving
You will say that you regret living in the past
The life you lived was long passed.
Companies see the fact
Hopefully make movies that reenact
What seems to be our past life
Another stab at our 80-year-old soul

Nostalgia creates a drug for this gen
I fight to look for the future while acknowledging
        my past
I want my life to feel more than lent
Tell nostalgia to go get bent.
In life I was not sent to live in the past
I was sent to build my future
You think disses and jokes are Savage
Well, nothing is more like that than to rise above
        the good feeling

Nostalgia is what you consider your spiritual upbringing
Cry about the good old days
On the verge of retiring?
No, then why do you keep resending that same feeling

You don't believe that nostalgia is a drug?
Then explain to me why all these memes show five
    years ago, when you played Black Ops 2?
Minecraft too?
Those Halo guardians still hold true.
It isn't enough when you are the only one doing it
You see the good feelings spilt
Down a darker alley,
Your brain telling nostalgia to git
When you do it with someone else, though, it's
    nothing but good
Your chemicals are reacting with
Someone else
It almost felt like you were there
Those memories you can share
Yet, when they leave
All you see is that moment in history
While your brain sits there and pleads
"Stay with me, we can make more memories, don't
    get lost again, this may be the last time
    I can get out of this cycle
Maybe to end the days and days of self-torment
I will grab this gun and pull the trigger"

Vision

I know what I've been told
The stories they barely unfold
The only thing I have is others' memories to recode
At such a young age my sibling would play
Hear the sounds of her laughter
Playing with Play-Doh clay.
My emotions displayed
They could be misinterpreted
Yet, the memories fade day after day.

The pictures and drawings still stand tall
Yet, my feelings for her only stand still or fall
I've hit another emotional wall
She never even got to see me crawl.

We are intertwined by nature
Yet I couldn't even hear you say my nomenclature.
I guess fate, yours had called
The step monster I have protection
You can't climb
It is ten feet tall.

As time fades
So does my grasp on reality
I don't even know if you got to hold and kiss me.
As my family puts the burden on lost me.
The accusations are funded egregiously
Your own mirror you can't stand to look in and see.
You claim I need grout
Yet, your foundation hasn't even started
I try to be happy
Yet, you want to destroy aggressively
Maybe it is time for the mirror to not be shattered
        and you admit that these are not my faults
Just someone else's or yours outwardly.
Why hate me?
The choice you made was to have me
The risk of the choice is known
Yet, you can't see the beauty
Just the clone of your eternal misery.

UNTITLED

What is the lowest point?
How many times can I be saved?
On the brink of insanity, enslaved?
Life is complex
Yet, all I feel is concaved
How do I make an imprint?
Do I surf now?
Or should I create my own waves?

Am I destined for greatness?
Or do I fall victim to the homeless embrace
To fall the victim's craze
Do I make it through?
Go to Pompeii too?
All I know is I've seen one end of the spectrum
Time to see the other one through.

Do I want to be comfortable?
It seems unlikely
Find comfort in life and do nothing spectacular
Shoo sheltered life.
Lest I live a normal time
I'll go crazy and grab a spectacular knife
I want to put all my chips on black
Make one detrimental spin
I will only know what to see
I don't want my chance to be once upon a time
When I had all the potential but I didn't do it on
        some sort of bullshit whim
I want to be great even if the chance is only slim.

To be on the embarking embrace
Time will only stand in its own place
Everything will freeze in a moment's time
I no longer want to hit the normal person's grind.
I don't see gray hairs yet
I will see them soon bet
Just like most aircrafts
You have to rebuild a rusted-up jet
I want this skill to be my passion
Better get my chance before what I have goes out
of fashion

We are so much alike are we?
The simple life is not made for me
I struggle with complacency
I don't know where to go to fulfill my destiny
I just know I suffer continuously.

LAYING IN MY LIES

I know I want to blame you
I know what lens I look through
The pain I feel is the only truth
Yet, all I wanna do is swing a bat and kill you

I am stuck in the past
In my mind graduation hasn't happened yet
What do I do to gain my own respect?
I have to let someone else trespass

My problems are my own
I am grown, yet I still don't know
Free and easy down the road I go?
I'm paddling
 against the current
Row, row, I always say, I just go with the flow

The tree outside looks very nice
Looking for help
I ask only thrice
Ending this cruel existence called life
I just listen to the pain
With helping hands I just create strife
Do I ever accept the help?
Or am I just asking for another belt?
Maybe, it's just my own survivors' guilt.

As each day passes
My worldview needs square-rimmed glasses
My world gets so small
My perspective and I
Fall on our asses
Am I the definition of what trash is?
My life just continues
I am the dummy that crash tests.
Describe it best, I can't do
This song and I
We are totally though

My problems are my own
I am grown, yet I still don't know
Free and easy down the road I go?
I'm paddling
 against the current
Row, row, I always say, I just go with the flow

BELIEF

We won't ever have this meeting, you and I
We will never see this problem eye to eye
Even with the drugs I still feel like I want to die
Here is the story, maybe you'll hear it as you're passing by

Shut up and listen
You are in court
Nothing you do will save you
Build yourself a safety fort
I said shut up, you nuisance, listen and hear
As I scream, this conversation I shall steer
Stay clear of answering his questions and just look and nod
That way he won't have a reason
You'll just act dumb and the insults won't be thrown
They'll be lobbed

What did you do on this fortnight?
Maybe around three?
I don't know, Dad (maybe I was spreading STDs)
You don't know?
How blatant can you be?
You obviously have something up your sleeve!
You are pitiful and stupid
Worth nothing to me
You might as well just stop trying and just leave
I hope you know this between your mother and me
I will end it, you will see
I won't even take the blame
I saved that for thee!

Sometimes it feels like the world's on my shoulders
Everyone's stomping on meeeee
Cuz sometimes it feels like the world's almost over
Why can't you just already kill meeee?

I see that you are improving slightly
Keep working hard and you'll make me proud
I wish he would have said that you better believe.
Instead he just brushes me off
Told me to try harder and just left it at that
No matter what kind of attention I tried to get it was
        never better than that
I don't want pity, I just want people to understand how
        I feel sometimes
No one wants to listen
Surely no one can help

You want to be successful, then heed my words
Stupid, worthless, killjoy, Debbie downer, fucking
        frowner, dick weed,
Fucking mush, you stupid steed, why do you constantly
        make an ass out of me?
You are the devil's child, my son, my only wish is that
        god sets you free from me
Let you be someone else's burden, they will surely see.
Of course, they will set me up for failure
Your words will surely succeed.
I just wanted someone to love me, you see.
I needed to stand up for myself and yet all you did was
        bury every part of me that is supposed to grow
        and I am afraid I will never live up to expectations
You buried the biggest part that was supposed to be
Now look at the masterpiece that will never, ever be
        completely me.
Thanks,
Sincerely me

UNKNOWN

As I try to breathe, I take a deep breath
Yet I only have shallow ones left
I don't recognize my own humble abode
I no longer know what is home.
I sit there and just hear a humming
Almost like a drone
I lay in fear
I don't know where my life
has gone left to steer
All I know left is now and here
I'm lost in the moment wanting to escape
Yet all I can do is leave my open mouth wide agape

FRANTIC

How do I take the first step?
Is the first the one to have leapt?
Is this where I get body checked?
I need to know the answers
My mind is still filled with these cancers
How do I meet my own criteria?
My own standards
How do I create my own manners?
How do I become one with the masters?
I shouldn't want that

I barely know the basics
How do I get from a greeting?
To smacking lips
I'd have a better chance if I just had a social issue
    to begin with
I'd rather have whispers and lisps
Crisper not cists
Swagger with a bit of soul
Not being shot down with crits
How do I ask the age-old question?
I have such a confession
I don't want my analysis to be an obsession
I just want a session
With such an age-old question
Yet, what keeps me drowning
Keeps me afloat
Do I abandon ship?
Do I jump out the boat?
What do I need for a perfect quote?
What does it matter?
I'll just choke

DRAWBACK

I wonder what words I say
I wonder who I am day after day
I went as far as gettin' a tray
Maybe there I should have stayed

The more I want to tell you
That amount I convince you
I wonder if it's me I'm telling
Not the medical queen
You are steady and surgical
I am too
You have strokes and steady hands
I have strokes with rhyming that few understand

All I am is a skid mark
I fill you up with emotions and then disappear
You take a chance, yet all I do is leave a smear
With no indication of where I am going
I make your life and mine unclear
I no longer know when I'm being sincere
I want to be near, yet I want to know what it's like to be free
Take my own steer

Life is unfair
Let's play in a diff-e-rent square
Take it by the horns
I'll never get a bat to hone
Do I have an extra chromosome?
I love you either way
Just picturing you old and gray
How do I attempt to live my life this way?
Life is unfair
Yeah, life is unfair

One day I fear that you will no longer play these games
You will go quietly and be defamed
Yet, you won't know the golden years
Since you will have a child
All you do is jeer
Yet, his future I will fear
I hope I am wrong
We both have that sixth sense on guessing
Yet, who will be wrong
Who will look like they're jesting?

Life is unfair
Let's play in a diff-e-rent square
Take it by the horns
You'll never look down on me
I'll try to have a loving and caring family
I love you either way
Just picturing you old and gray
How do I attempt to live my life this way?
Life is unfair
Yeah, life is unfair

There are just some things I can't admit, I just don't
    know where to omit I need my life to get
    through the lenses, I have yet to see through
    my indecisions on the curb I'm ready to follow
    my journey and see this through, if nothing else
    I'll write a book and leave these inside.
Somehow, I have to confide my feelings or I'll go crazy.
Life is unfair, yet I am gonna try to barrel through

REWIND

To feel what I feel now is something dreamy
I used to feel only gloom and doom
Only such is dreary
My body no longer feels weary.

I feel 20 again
Yet, I can still write with my imaginary pen
I have never known what life could entail
If I ever did get one over
I never knew with a little bit of help I could possibly prevail
Maybe I can shed pounds
Maybe I can be away from Clifford
Smaller in scale

No one knows the path that I chose
Maybe I will see a brighter side
My lens is not ready to be replaced
I am not ready to die
Solving mysteries
With nothing but curiosity to quench
I will know better by which to smell
Depression's stench
One aspect at a time to improve
Maybe this time I will be able to finish my next move

I can finally write a new chapter
Nothing as easy as happily ever after
I won't walk with a slouch
I will no longer be what we portrayed Pa to be
We will not be the grouch
I will not be ridden to a couch
Mr. Grinch had the pole and cut it down to 2 feet tall
Now I will work my own kind of magic
Squeezing through the chimney hole
Maybe I finally beat the hard level and got a Candy Crush scroll

I have unlimited boost
I have 99 lives
I will no longer sit down and silently cry
A good line I just heard
The words that come out weren't mine
Yet, I was lost
It took me just a little bit of time
Life still isn't easy
That much I know for sure
Yet, I feel less queasy
I'll fast track to success
Depression will only tease me.

No one knows the path that I chose
Maybe I will see a brighter side
My lens is not ready to be replaced
I am not ready to die
Solving mysteries
With nothing but curiosity to quench
I will know better by which to smell
Depression's stench
One aspect at a time to improve
Maybe this time I will be able to finish my next move

A second chance to start over
Is this what it's like to send someone over?
Changing teams like a flip of the switch
Maybe I can have the curiosity of Lilo and Stitch.

Everyone in life wants to be young
Yet, I feel like I got my spring sprung
Leap year to jump forward no more
I feel five years younger
An old man no more.
"I wish I was young again"
Not everything is granted
Depression is anti
And I am less psychotic
Who knew playing with kinetic sand?
At my age would be unironic
Age doesn't define me
I want to still live my best
The whole world is again in front of me
Let's take this next step.

No one knows the path that I chose
Maybe I will see a brighter side
My lens is not ready to be replaced
I am not ready to die
Solving mysteries
With nothing but curiosity to quench
I will know better by which to smell
Depression's stench
One aspect at a time to improve
Maybe this time I will be able to finish my next move

BLOCK

Alone in the dark
I was fallin' apart
Nothin' to save me
Except this dying art
Where does this music even start?

When I was young
I knew I wanted to be just like Mom
Vettin' the animals
Wanting them to go back to instinct
My rhymes and myself aren't in sync
Tell me why, N*SYNC
Tell me why I hear all this whispering
What's blocking my path?
I can't just take another hot bath
I wrote about it
But will anyone ever hear my wrath?
Sometimes I wish I was punk
Almost lose it all with staph

I don't know what you did
Brought me home
A chapter we go back and see
Hopefully it's the last they see of me
Trying to get this dead heart to beat
I have a couple scars that run so deep
Why can't anyone listen?
I got these stories
I swear I didn't cheat!

Another song down the drain
When am I gonna stop listenin' to my brain?
How else am I goin' to be i n s a n e?
Insane
My membrane to train
One minute it's with me
Next it's in Spain
Now that I'm on pills
It's even harder to sustain
There isn't much left of my crane-ium
My neurons,
Like me have no self-respect
Just a disconnect
Yet, I sit here and fret
What is the next step?
I hope I don't forget

The words I still hear
They grip me like a hand
Choking me to submission
A needle prodding me
Just like a tiny incision
One day it's Destroy All Humans
The next is love is unconditional
Then I guess that pain is unequivocal
I just wish my brain
Could be somewhere more
Asymmetrical
Who said that?
Where did they go?
Did you hear that as well?
Another voice again
I wish it was everyone else, parallel.

As I speak my final words of grace
Should I spread more hate?
Yet, all we do is fall in this hole
Just like the voice said
Asymmetrical

AFRAID

What am I afraid of?
Getting older every day?
Feeling this pit in my stomach
Day after day
Or is it something more sinister
Much to my dismay
Ignorance is bliss
Now my notion to sway

Is it more sinister?
To not understand me
Your own son?
On any day
I need help
Adittionally, all you do is make it worse
Take a minute to understand
I want to be happy
Yet, I want to feel the darkness
Overwhelming
At least in its touch
The voices at least hear my pleas
You just turn me down upright
Instantaneously
Yet, all I can do is be in silence and write

You continue to write
With no one to hear
Another hit my battleship
Nope, just an emotional spear.
To stay young is my wish
Further it is impossible to come true
How do I grow old gracefully?
So many others do
To the last part I will write
The notion again to sway

I hear laughter in the distance
Further I hear a distortion
The green you see
Is the grey I saw
Gingers might not have a soul
Where is my real one?
As everyone has fun
I feel death's clock ticking
Afraid to do too much
At the cost of my life
Further I do know
That not living is death anyways
How do I live, not without fear?
But the ability to overcome
Conquer, see through it to the end
Honestly, how much further can I bend?

SABOTAGE

Sometimes it is the demons that are lurking that
hurt the most, not the ones that face you head on
(idea for sure)

You look me in the eyes
"Be what you want to be"
You really believe that?
Or is this something else I should ignore?

Another check next to unknown
Nobody gets me
I'm all alone
I should rely on you
Next to nothing for sure
I want to be accepted
Moreover I'm just part of the nexus
Where is my Corre?

Another round of disgrace
Another chance to mourn
My freedom is at stake
What I like is a waste
I want to make my own rules
Post-haste
I wish the front lines of battle
Were the only ones I fought
Additionally you now have shown
I need to keep my head on a swivel
Your chance to hear a glorious thing
Has gone to waste
I think and I thunk
You think I'm just a normie flunk
No good at sports
Especially a dunk
No good at school
Guess I'm just a punk.
I guess I'm not meant to be happy
The demons behind me make sure.

You both epitomize polar opposites
Formerly the more I hate I spew
My father doesn't hear brew
The more love I force upon you
Yet all the love granted for you
There only lays waste
Underneath a fake green paste.
I love you,
Formerly you stabbed me in the back
At least him and I tried in the front
You were seething,
While we both grunt.
(She says to ask for help yet you asked at 17,
    make that part of the next verse(s))
You told me to ask for help
To involve you next time
When I asked for help at 17
You told me
I didn't need help
That knife was a pussy move
Yet, at 25
I show worsening symptoms
You show resentment
My feelings show no respite
Despite for love
You just bury your head
Resting a bit
Ignore while I sit
Mourn another passing day
I am already dead
The motions I move
Nothing else will ever sooth
You just want me to be happy
Just being here
I want to leave
Left seething like before
My head is just so damn sore

INSANITY

Everyone has voices in their head
They lay to rest
Only in bed
Mine are forever awake
Running their own games
Running their feelings
Like Drake

You act like it isn't there
Lurking just beneath the surface
Twisting your neck
Never showing your true side
Like Saw, but on purpose

Maybe your demons go as far as
"I hope they call off"
My thoughts go as far as
"I hope their insides are in a pig trough"

Your demons sleep so well
I hear that I should swallow some bleach
Sometimes I think help is outside of reach

"Maybe I should stop at this hill
Just deep throat a bunch of pills"

AFRAID

Teach me to get my ability back
I want to get me back
I want to force each and every rhyme
I want it to flow with each passing line

I just want to express myself
Overthink too much
Live free and die hard
Writing is my passion
Going until I die
Capacity shows a shelf life
Very few get past father time
Have to rhyme every line
I have to have it flow
Each passing time
The block I have
Creates such frustration
My idea of writing
Is a misconception

I have a saddle on my own life
I just get bit
Held back
Told lies
This song is for passing
My mind is gassing
I can't see clearly

The more clear everything seems to be
The less I can write
The less I can see
My passion seeps through
My finger cracks
The writing I drew
The hope I have for the future
Leaves as quick as morning dew

Just earlier this year I could write 4 times a week
Now I am surprised if I can write something incomplete
The stress on my life becomes so much more
Living at home
Destruction at its core

RETURN

I never wanted to think this
I never wanted to say
At times like these
I consider going to pray

You haven't changed one bit
People see you differently
Living with you again
You treat everyone as you treat yourself
Internally, you create falsehoods
You overthink too much
As my past catches up to me
In more ways than one
I'll be someone's brightest day
One day I'll be their sun.

The sins I bring about
Are not easily repaired
We all hold grudges
That's why we live in despair
As my clouds disperse
I wonder if I'll ever write another good verse
I do wonder
Which is worse
I can't believe I say this
How did I become more of a man than you?
I guess man isn't the right way to put it
Human seems a better fit
You are the dragon
Furthermore, I will not slay
Putting you out of your misery
That's just the easy way
I want you to know
I found an alternate path
Soon I will no longer hear
Your breadths will not reach to me
The wrath I soon will be unfit
Another note I will sift

FACE-OFF

I feel so numb
There are days that
With the medicine
I feel happy
I feel as though
I can accept myself
As the demons are swallowed back down
I come to realize
Who am I?
I just have what used to be
Grasping at the past
Halt! Who goes there?

As my mind tries to think of what to say next
I grasp at the easy-flow intent
Where I get lost
The feelings intense
Now I just grab at anything

I feel so dead on the inside
I try to resist the urge of a weed high
Knowing I make some fire music
Now I feel inspired
Just as quickly as an idea pops up
Creativity locks up
Now that passion has fired on every cylinder
I'm just the jester's villager
Sit and wait

My patience like the Bering Strait
As poems get shorter
I walk on eggshells
When I was smoking weed
I could say things out loud
Saying things loud and proud
Now it's clear
I'm too closed off and afraid
Each word said
Is just a shot blank
It kills me
Point blank
Where are the rhymes
Where I talk about backstabbing
A shiv or shank
Look, there's a skank
I just know right now I have nothing left
I just want to curl into a ball
Looks like I'll brawl
Better Call Saul
That series is dead
It explains me
That's what it is
I'm dead
13 Reasons Why
I made a suicide reference
Man, not being able to write
I just want to die

Hellfire

In my mind I feel so numb
Back with my parents again
It never seemed fun
Scolded and attacked
At each corner I turn
To be continuously lied to
Makes it a concern
You can't control how I feel anymore
There is no peace corps
Raiding my space like 51
Getting shot down
With gunner's delight
A machine gun killing everyone in sight
I know I've said everyone has their breaking point
I think I'm hitting close to mine
There isn't much time left to tell
Both turns happen
I'm going to hell
As I contemplate suicide
Another thought comes to mind
What if instead of offing me
And ending it all

I end other people's happiness
That is all
I'm too afraid to go try
Thoughts are one thing
Facing it is beyond my fathomable mind
hate what I've become
Too afraid to learn how to shoot a gun
Kill myself with every ounce of my being
Instead I might just kill for fun
I can be the judge
Give people hope

Or just shoot them, saying "nope"
I am desperate to feel alive
Just trying not to be on the other side
Too much has happened to try and forgive
I want to grab a prisoner's shiv
Watch the light fade
Killing everyone showing shade
I can't fathom getting any older
I am scared of what the next day will bring
Lights shining so shimmering
Just like this blade
All these colors might as well be black and grey
I know the colors will show what I already see
A dark at best dim future
Barely held on by a crafter's suture
just want to be happy
I crave it with very being
Maybe I won't be happy
Until I feel alive
Censor myself?
Are you crazy?
I'll shoot up a school
And suffocate a baby
The thoughts they drive me
More want sin
I might lose my mind
With just one shot of gin
Maybe that's too generic
Arson eccentric
Lead the world to number 3
I'm artistic too
Let's see how much destruction people truly seek
A record to want to break
No one's ever accomplished genocide

With just a wisp of my hand
I can be an emperor Jedi
One hand out and people start to choke
Once my reign is finally over I'll be old and dreary
Cyanide and happiness
Oh, very clearly.
Push me over the edge and see what happens
Everyone has their limits
Are you willing to find mine?
I'm deceptive
You wouldn't know at first glance
I show you what I want you to see
Quiet and kept to myself
One day you will see
What is truly underneath

Get a clue?
I hear you
The voices tell me
They must be telling the truth
I hear the past
That's why I can't escape it
Worthless piece of shit

LOST AND RELOCATED

I hear the whispers and they gently wisp in the wind
I can only hear the clear whispers of sin
Yet, they do not blow by me
I hear their voices creakin'
Let me out!
Yet, they stay put and drive me bad
Now others shall feel my pain
Lest it drives them mad

You might think this a confession
This will be utmost
I'll make you sad
Although, everyone I can't get
The years that run by
I'll be sure most know
Dad knows best
Lest we forget
Blood doesn't give a person that title
Raising them has.
They don't want to be raised by me
That story is sad
Lest I kill years off their life
Like my dad has

I'm a man of simple needs
Not one for greed
No need for a loud stampede
Just simply time consuming
Math, if you please

I try to do everything for these kids
Yet, all they do is plead
"When can we go home?"
4 years and 20 days left indeed
Soon you will know what life is like for me
Wasting away in sorrow
Distant thoughts
Ear-piercing screams
It's almost music to my ears

Go visit my sickly mother in the nursing home
She gleams and glees over me
Making me feel at unease
Knowing that the kids frightened
Is my only medicine
A mount on the wall
Kids have to kneel and pray
On the animal rug
Single lines
Single crimes
The mat isn't leather
Though leathery
The stench and the screams
The drugs and the dreams
They all make me at peace, tranquility

2 years left and you can go home
They get crafty and use birds as drones
They know my location
Yet, why haven't they come?
Do they think I'm dumb?
They must feel what I felt
I wear my father's skin, the rug
As a pelt.
As my mother gets too old to remember
They think she has gone mad
But look out

The dream has now become a nightmare
My mom is a saint
She would help anybody
At least try
Now her gleeful invitations forefront
Have turned to terrible cries
As the staff have to strap her down
Even though they have been outlawed
Maybe one more dream will be met
Before I reach my downfall
Electrotherapy
Has its 100-year reunion
I claim to the union she is not fit for her own decisions
They sign the decisions over to me
Finally at peace once again
The devil sits there, laughs at the deeds I have done
    in his place
I leave nothing of my destruction
Not even a trace
I have never thought about what name I should have
Yet, I am always forgotten
I am a mist
You just keep walkin'
I am there
You do notice
You just walk right on through
Shooting only a glance
Nightmare fuel
Be careful of my reign of terror
Or your kids will be abducted too.

BATTLES AND WARS

Everything you want
This is what you need
I can finally be your steed
Trample me
Further, the fear that withstands hope
Is stronger in me
Nay to medicine
I'd rather just croak
Keel over and lie
I don't know if my mind's state will ever consider me
    getting a piece of the pie
All you have to do is try
Put in some effort
Hey, look, don't cry
Here is a participation trophy
Nowadays, you get that
You can't get it from your kids
Pried away
Lest you hurt their feelings
Much to everyone's fragile dismay
America has won every battle and scoured every war
Yet, Vietnam was not a W
Just an L for sure

I hear the voices as they talk to me loud
My battles may have won
It just feels like 'Nam in my head
Everyone fights their own war
A long time I thought it was the Civil War
Part of me wins and part of me loses
We live in holy matrimony
However the wars that are fought
History has appeared
America and I

We both digress
Our congress sees this war as a blemish
A mere pest
Imperfections cannot be tolerated
We must help everyone else
While our country is in shambles
Deteriorated
Covering up what hurts most
Keep pushed down
Like kids in a pool playing around
Yet, whose head is being put under?
Is it me or what is covered?
I guess time will tell
Life's full of blunders
I can't help but think
How much oxygen do I have left?
Or am I strong enough to keep it from surfacing
I hear the murmuring
It tells me to kill
Although I am not a serial killer
Suicide watch
Guess I better turn the happiness up one more notch
Another pill will keep me sober
I should see greens and blues and purples
Futhermore all I see is gray, black and no silvers
Just a sliver of hope as life rotates once again
Is there nobody to save me
My demons I must befriend?
1000 downers and drowsy
Sounds like just my speed
My thoughts were better organized
When I was just chillin' and smokin' weed.

LOVE OR ACCEPTANCE

This might have poemesque-type rhymes and rhythms, but I'll mostly be just talking. Maybe it will be a full poem later.

My process is that I hunger for both love and acceptance. In my experience the earlier years you want affection, you want love. You crave love because you are growing and learning and you need a helping hand. You are dependent on that love and affection. When you don't get the love and admiration from one or both of your parents you tend to lash out, to grab the attention. You want them to realize that you exist, any sort of attention negative or positive shows that they care at all. If they are yelling at you and screaming at you at least you have their attention. Maybe they will notice your hunger. You hope they do, because you don't know why you lash out more than being noticed, you think you are a bad kid, a bad child. Being ignored is hurtful and resentful. It shows they would rather ignore you than even consider helping or fixing the situation. I want you to notice that me saying at 6 that Grandpa and Grandma will like my sister's letter more than mine. You didn't see the signs. I noticed the signs when it was too late to catch them. How was I supposed to know? I was a child, I didn't understand.

In the teenage years, you still crave that love, but you show it in different ways. Maybe if they accept you as worthy, love will soon follow. You want them to notice your accomplishments, and your drive. When you don't notice that, when even with our best efforts you don't want to even show us acceptance we give up and fall into depression. Without proper guidance for your kids they will grow up an emotional mess. It could drive us to be creepy or drive us to force love and acceptance. That is not something any kid deserves. Even if they know right and wrong, that animosity kicks in and they can't help it. It is absolutely disgusting that you planted a seed for the possible monster. When they know right and wrong and choose wrong that is their fault. How you raise them to crave that much to force it, that is the wrongdoing of being raised. They were raised wrong so they chose wrong. Nothing is that black and white. Some people conquer that problem and become better people. Sometimes it is that black and white. Sometimes they become their worst selves.

Knowing both of those, because I have been on both of those spectrums, what makes you think I want you in my life? That I want your help? Swallow my pride and ask for your help? Are you serious? I want you out of my life. The trauma in my life and knowing that you don't believe anything I do or put my mind to shows that I not only can't ask for your help, I would be stupid to even consider asking you for anything. You want to repair what we have now? You told me when I was 10 that I burned bridges between you and I. I was fucking 10. I can go through so much shut that I had problems with at age 10. At age 10 I was still wearing diapers. At age 10 I wanted to stab my temple with a butter knife in front of my sister and my best friend. At age 10 you loved me less than the Oakland Raiders. At age 10 I was labeled the bad kid. I was labeled the failure, the outcast, the nothing. 15 years later and I still struggle with my identity and my confidence/self-esteem. I am emotionally immature. When I compliment people or open up to people or ask them to help me. I am creepy and shunned away. I ask questions because I am innocent not because I am weird and perverted. You want me to ask you for help? At age 16 I asked if you could show me how much cologne I should put on so I wouldn't be told I smell bad at school. You didn't take the 30 seconds to help me. At age 18 when I told you that my gf told me she would rather spend time with her other guy friend than me her bf on my birthday. It was my fault for being overweight. I weighed 210 was in marching band carrying the biggest bass drum in drumline, was in 4 different clubs including Ultimate Frisbee and on top of that getting straight A's before that as well it was my fault for being overweight? I had muscle. I had a stomach because of my cancer and the fact that my muscles were ripped to shreds. I don't think it is possible to even get abs. My fault. You wanted to force your wife to choose between you and me. And told her if she chose me that you would divorce her and blame the divorce on me. My fault. I am emotionally destroyed and I don't think I'll ever find live anywhere. You destroyed me emotionally. I either underreact or overreact. Whenever you yelled at me for doing something wrong I could never stand up for myself. Look and nod. "You don't have any balls," you conditioned me not to have any balls, you fucking idiot. You don't know your own destruction. Now I take your insults with a grain of salt. I'm the idiot? You spent 15 years breaking me down. I've spent only the last 2 years building myself back up. You don't understand why I am like this? You should question, why are you like this?

JOHN

I want to say this straight
No rhymes
No silly inquisitions
Or little jokes in the lines.
Just man to man.

You showed me something I never thought I could see.
You went the extra mile to make sure I was appreciated
You complimented me when no one else would.
You gave love to a brother who didn't know what love meant
It was "money" well spent (spending money takes time,
    I just know you wasted your investment on me, and
    paid off diligently) I want to thank you from the
    bottom of my misconstrued heart
However, misunderstood I am
Or how dark I get and let the demons come out to play
You never let me go astray
See, I didn't want it to be rhyming
I just can't help it
Maybe this is how it's paid back
Just sway.
Don't let the picture get taken away.
For once in my life I'm like the 1950s version of gay.
Happy

This poem won't go out of this day (this is special,
    just between me and you) you can share it with
    who you want, but once I give this to you it is yours.
You deserve all the happiness in the world
I don't see color, I see souls
Brother, your soul has zero holes.
I would still be wallowing in my own fear and
    depression if it weren't for people like you
With all the demons that are in the world
I'm glad an angel like you floats in this world.
I know what love feels like
I know the standard I need to hold myself
I know what you have done for me, but what have
    I done for you?
Mr. Scrooge usually
Tonight I am fearful
With just a little push
I can be brave through the challenges and fear
I'm Scooby-Dooby-Doo.
I don't say this often
It isn't for the faint of heart
I trust you.
I hope you succeed in all that you do.
I also hope Amanda loves you as much as I love myself now too.

PUSH AND PULL

She runs away to avoid getting disappointed
He runs his mouth and gets in trouble again
You pushed me away to no end
And just as I fall off you pull me up and try to pull me in
How do you believe I will respond?
My ideals have grown too fond
You think the bridges burned
Are over a pond
What you don't know
Is that you are wrong
The bridge that would be burned
Would go from here to Vietnam
I'm having flashbacks
And you are the cause
Roles reversed
You pull
And I push you away
How else should I respond?

Te-e-e-en years of pain and discomfort
Of being pushed away
Slammed down and hit as the force of a cupboard
No second thought as to the noise that has plundered
Only grab what's on the inside
Emptied out
Now you want to restock?
Bitch, you thought.
As you reach out
I push off and you pull me back in fear

I don't have any bridges to mend
All I do is overthink, pretend and defend
I fear for your safety
Now I must offend
Stoic am I
Po-e tree I want to dismemb-er
I am not your son, nor your friend
I have to push down how I really feel
These wounds are deep
It isn't like anything else
Yet, maybe this will finally die
We can move onto a new trend

My pain is but a distant memory
As new people enter my life
I'm not 2-wheeled yet,
But four wheels I no longer like
As I learn to balance better
Maybe, I can stop riding this trike
Maybe, one day soon
I could have my very own bike.

I can't be the person you fall onto
You pull me closer and I just push away,
Astray. Who, though?
That's the question blundered
I hate to see what can still be mended
Yet, if I say how I really feel
Will you then become 6 feet under?
Will I be the groundskeeper?
As you go into madness deeper?
The mind plays games
Yet, all I speak is truth
We no longer have innocent's youth

I don't have any bridges to mend
All I do is overthink, pretend and defend
I fear for your safety
Now I must offend
Stoic am I
Po-e tree I want to dismemb-er
I am not your son, nor your friend
I have to push down how I really feel
These wounds are deep
It isn't like anything else
Yet, maybe this will finally die
We can move onto a new trend

Will you be 6 feet under?
Or will you be 6 feet recovered?